THE ABCs OF C.B.T.

COGNITIVE BEHAVIOR THERAPY

A Professional School Counselor's Guide
To Help Students in Grades 3-8 Help Themselves

WRITTEN BY
Kathie Guild
PROFESSIONAL SCHOOL COUNSELOR, NBCT

ABOUT THE AUTHOR

Kathie Guild is currently an elementary school counselor in Chapel Hill, NC. She taught 4th grade and kindergarten in Kansas and New York before moving to Budigen, Germany where she worked as a school counselor in the Department of Defense Dependent School System. Kathie routinely presents at the N.C. School Counselor's State Conference and to graduate students in the U.N.C. Counseling Education Department. She is a Nationally Board Certified Teacher in School Counseling (N.B.C.T.). Her other works include *Froggy and Friends, Froggy and Friends II*, *More Froggy and Friends, Everyone's Included, How to Stop Before You Pop*, and *Just Say It*.

kathieguild.weebly.com

The A.B.C.s of C.B.T.

Softcover ISBN: 978-1-57543-318-9

Reprinted 2019
Distributed by YouthLight
PO Box 115
Chapin, SC 29036
Phone: 1-803-345-1070
https://www.youthlight.com

Graphic images: 123rf.com and shutterstock.com

Printed in the U.S.A.

Contents

A NOTE FROM THE AUTHOR

The A.B.C.s of C.B.T. program was developed through my intensive work with students in a school setting using Cognitive Behavior Therapy. This program is best presented in sequential order. It is recommended that the students master each component before advancing to the next step.

As a way for children to relate to Aaron Beck's unhelpful thinking styles, I created cartoon characters to represent the classic cognitive biases formulated by C.B.T. The C.B.T. animal characters help explain to the students that they are their own worst critics, and in the words of Anaïs Nin:

"We don't see things as they are, we see them as we are."

The A.B.C.s of C.B.T. program is best suited for students in Grades 3-8, and is organized into three sections.

The first section, *The Counselor's Guide to Cognitive Behavior Therapy*, is organized into chapters that provide an overview of the principles and learning objectives behind C.B.T.

The second section, *Teaching Cognitive Behavior Therapy to Students*, offers eight lessons to teach students the building blocks of C.B.T. and optional activities. The lessons take from 30-45 minutes each and should be presented in sequential order.

The last section contains the reproducible worksheets and mini-posters. These pages can also be downloaded in color.

TO ACCESS THIS BOOK'S DIGITAL CONTENT VISIT:

https://youthlight.com/digitalDownload.php?id=3301

Enter password: AB0171_digital

This file will download in the zip file format (.zip). A zip file is a single file containing one or more compressed files. You may need a program or app such as WinZip® to unzip, open and extract the content. (Most computers, tablets and mobile devices have built in tools to extract and manage .zip files.)

The Counselor's Guide To Cognitive Behavior Therapy (C.B.T.)

CHAPTER 1

Introduction and Overview of C.B.T.

This curriculum is based on the principles of Cognitive Behavior Therapy (C.B.T.) developed by American psychiatrist Aaron Beck in the 1960s. In his work with depressed patients, Beck noted patients experiencing a steady flow of negative thoughts about themselves, the world, and the future. These unhelpful thoughts were automatic and spontaneous in nature. Patients spent little to no time reflecting on their automatic thoughts, and thus the distorted thoughts were viewed as valid.

Beck developed C.B.T. as an alternative approach to the dominant therapies at the time largely falling into three schools of thought:

- B.F. Skinner's Behaviorism
- Sigmund Freud's Psychoanalysis
- Carl Rogers' Person-Centered Approach

Albert Ellis' Rational Emotive Therapy, which began in the 1950s, had some influence on Beck, but Beck diverged with Ellis' practice of telling the patients what he believed was going on. Beck felt that patients themselves should explore their distorted thoughts through the use of Socratic questioning.

Cognitive Behavior Therapy is an effective counseling approach to use in a school setting due primarily to its practicality and ease of implementation. An added benefit of C.B.T. for the school counselor is the time-limited design. The principles of C.B.T. can be taught to students and mastered in between 6-12 sessions. With C.B.T., the focus is on the present with an orientation towards problem-solving through Socratic questioning. Students learn specific skills to implement not only for their present situations, but for future problems as well.

Central to C.B.T. is teaching students four specific self-help skills:

1. Recognizing and identifying distorted thinking
2. Modifying or changing thoughts
3. Relating and reacting to others in different ways
4. Changing or adapting behaviors

C.B.T. is both directive and instructional. The counselor and student form an alliance that mirrors a working collaborative relationship. The theory makes good use of Socratic questioning in order for the students to examine and evaluate their unhelpful patterns of thinking. The school counselor guides the students in identifying and changing their distressing thoughts. In addition, the students practice flexible ways of not only thinking, but of responding to those vexing thoughts.

There are two underlying assumptions central to Cognitive Behavior Therapy:

1. Students are fully capable of recognizing and changing their own thoughts, feelings, and behaviors.
2. Some thoughts might be distorted and fail to accurately reflect reality.

Another distinguishing feature of Cognitive Behavior Therapy is the recognition and emphasis distorted thinking has on one's physiology. Students are taught to pay attention to the physical symptoms that often accompany thoughts such as a racing heart beat, pounding in the head, ringing in the ears, a dry mouth, grinding of teeth, a feeling of having butterflies in the stomach, rapid breathing, feeling flushed, and so on. C.B.T. acts as a type of biofeedback by connecting an important link between the mind and the body.

This program's lessons are written for presentation to small groups. However, the lessons can be used just as effectively with individuals or in classroom guidance.

A Pre- and Post-Test (page 52) is included to measure the learning received during the sessions. By comparing each student's test results from the first lesson and the last lesson, the counselor can analyze the program's effectiveness and determine if any student needs additional help. These results can also serve to validate the program and provide data to support the program.

NAME ______________________ DATE ______________

The A.B.C.s of C.B.T.

PRE- and POST-TEST

CIRCLE YOUR ANSWER	TRUE	FALSE
1. We have thoughts before we have feelings.	T	F
2. You can control your feelings by focusing on your thoughts.	T	F
3. I am familiar with and can name all 11 of the C.B.T. animal characters.	T	F
4. In the A.B.C. model of C.B.T., B stands for behavior.	T	F
5. The Insidious Shadow represents the unknown or the "what ifs" of life.	T	F
6. A dogmatic thought creates anxiety, and is persistent and reoccurring.	T	F
7. Steps D and E of the A.B.C.D.E.F. model of C.B.T. involve questioning and scrutinizing one's distressing thoughts.	T	F
8. Scaling, in C.B.T., means how much you weigh.	T	F
9. Our emotions produce physical sensations.	T	F
10. I know many ways to regulate my feelings and behaviors, and how to change and rethink my unhelpful thoughts.	T	F

52 **The A.B.C.s of C.B.T.** © 2017 Mar·co Products, Inc. 1-800-448-2197

CHAPTER 2

Optional Pre-Teaching of Skill-Building Activities

Some students are able to quickly grasp the concept that they are the creators of their own upsetting thoughts. These students have insight into their feelings and behaviors, but feel powerless to stop distressing thoughts from happening. The framework of Cognitive Behavior Therapy (C.B.T.) empowers these students to achieve mastery over their thoughts and subsequent feelings and actions. Other students may need to be taught or have a review of certain skills in order for them to successfully learn and utilize the principle self-help skills central to C.B.T. By pre-teaching fundamental constructs on feelings, self-regulation, perspective/perception, fact versus opinion, and actions and reactions, the foundation for C.B.T. will be strengthened.

Feelings (ACTIVITY: PAGE 22)

The basic building block in C.B.T., as in most counseling theories, is grappling with the diversity of human emotions. Students have to be taught to first identify what they are feeling, and then how to express those feelings in a positive way. That is, the expression of a person's feelings does not harm oneself or others. Reading picture books, watching or performing puppet shows, and/or watching short videos on feelings is time well spent. Students need to comprehend that every feeling serves a purpose, and that there are appropriate ways of displaying and managing emotions. Feelings should not be suppressed. Feelings should be expressed, but in ways that do not have negative consequences. Presenting lessons on feelings will help the students as they complete step C of the *Simple A.B.C. Worksheet*, and scale they way the are feeling on the 1-5 Likert Scale. In the *Resources* section on page 80, you will find suggested books and movies on the topic of feelings.

Self-Regulation Color Wheel (ACTIVITY: PAGE 23 – WORKSHEET: PAGES 53-54)

There is a wealth of information associated with linking feelings and/or moods to colors (color psychology). The Disney movie, *Inside Out,* explored this concept, examining the emotional life of a young girl as she navigated a few difficult days in her life. Different situations evoke different moods and/or feelings, and moving from feeling to feeling (color to color) throughout the day is both common and human.

The *Self-Regulation Color Wheel* (page 53) can be introduced once the students have mastered the expression of feelings. The wheel has six colors (three primary and three secondary colors) that blend into one another:

Purple = listless, no energy, lazy, lethargic, slow
Blue = passive, relaxed, dreamy
Green = balance, calm, ready to learn
Yellow = high energy, excited, agitated or restless, alert
Orange = heightened state, revved up, frustrated
Red = tense, charged up, strong surge of emotion, anger

The circular shape is significant in that it shows the continuity and fluidity of human existence. The *Self-Regulation Color Wheel* is a great visual tool to help the students understand that being able to adapt their temperament (color) to the situation will translate into competency in social situations.

The orange and red colors signify an elevated or heightened state. Yellow signifies nervous energy, blue is relaxed and languid, and purple listless and inactive. The color green represents a state of being where temperament is balanced. Green signifies not too much or too little energy, and is optimal for learning.

Discuss with the students the different colors and associated feelings. Then discuss what colors (temperaments) are best suited for different situations they encounter. For example, ask:

What "color" might be best in order to learn in school?
What "color" might be best at a friend's sleepover?
What "color" might be best on the playground?
What "color" might be best at home after dinner?

Continue the lesson by exploring different situations. Have the students practice articulating what "color" they would be in each situation, then identifying things they can do or say to move along the circle until they are at a "color" that feels best for that particular situation.

It is important to stress that people have different temperaments. Some people are in a yellow state most of the time, while other people are in a blue state and remain calm and steady. The colors do not represent good or bad attitudes or behaviors. For example, before or during a competition, being revved or charged up (orange) provides a player with the required motivation and energy.

On the back of the *Self-Regulation Color Wheel* (page 54), have the students list people, places, things, and activities that help them remain calm or make them feel better.

The color wheel lesson will help guide the students as they complete the C.B.T. worksheets, especially in the D.E.F. sections. When students rethink disconcerting thoughts by disputing them (searching for evidence for and against), they are in essence moving along the color wheel to a more balanced mindset.

Perspective (ACTIVITY: PAGE 23)

Perspective and perception are important conceptual skills for students to acquire. Understanding and accepting that others might see things in a completely different light than you is an important life-skill. Not everything is black or white, right or wrong, empty or full. Some things fall into gray areas, and students who can live with and accept that variants of gray exist will fare better when things don't go as planned.

Have the students stand in three different places in a room (front, back, side), then ask them to name the things that they see. Discuss how, depending on where they stood, certain objects were more noticeable/obvious. Then ask the students which view was correct? Relate this activity to how people can view events, conflicts, and life in general from different perspectives. Being able to see things from another person's perspective is an important life-skill. When we challenge and question our perceptions, we become more accepting of others and are better able to handle distressing events and conflicts that may arise.

There are many free images available Online (search for 3D optical illusions and depth perception illusions) that help illustrate the concept of perspective. Google Earth is a fun way to have the students view the world from different vantage points.

Lessons on perspective will help the students as they complete step E (evaluating) on the worksheets.

Fact or Opinion? (ACTIVITY: PAGE 24 – WORKSHEET: PAGE 55)

Closely associated with perspective and perception is being able to discern the difference between facts and opinions. Discuss with the students the difference between facts and opinions. Facts can be proven. A fact is something that actually exists, the truth. Opinions are judgments or personal views. Opinions fall short of absolute certainty. Use the *Fact or Opinion?* worksheet (page 55) to reinforce this lesson.

Actions and Reactions (ACTIVITY: PAGE 24 – WORKSHEETS: PAGES 56-57)

Once the students understand perspective and perception and facts versus opinions, they are ready to move on to the concept of *actions* (events) and *reactions* (how much those events impact us). For some students, every action (event) is met with the same or a similar reaction. Not being called on in class or not being selected as the student of the week becomes a catastrophe, a life-changing event with extreme displays of inconsolable emotion (hysterical crying, throwing, yelling). Students need to be taught that the size or scope of the reaction should be proportionate to the size or scope of the action (event). Small actions, such as a friend sitting with someone you don't like or forgetting your homework, can be disappointing, but they are not a 911 emergencies. A good example of a large reaction to a small action (event) is a young child in a store throwing a tantrum when a parent refuses to buy him or her a toy or candy. This is a small problem, and the child's overreaction is out of proportion to the situation.

Review the *Actions and Reactions* worksheet (page 56) with the students. Discuss which events are considered small, medium, and large actions. Expand the lesson using the *More About Actions and Reactions* worksheet (page 57).

CHAPTER 3

A.B.C. Thoughts

Thoughts take star billing in Cognitive Behavior Theory. These thoughts form a triangular A.B.C. pattern.

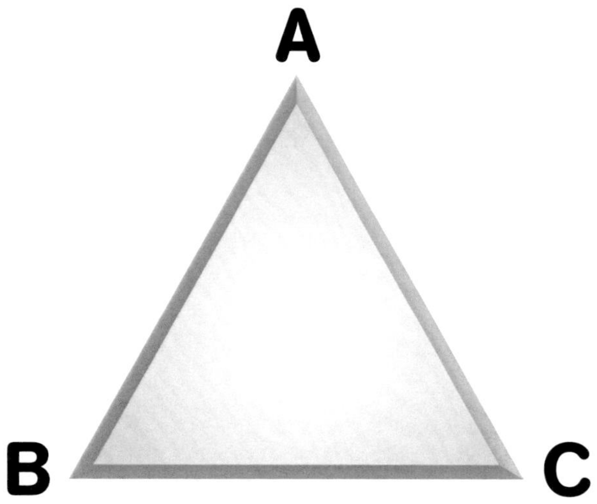

A = Activating or actual event

B = Belief or automatic thought about the event

C = Consequences (feelings and behaviors resulting from the thought)

The actual event (A) is neutral, impartial, and devoid of meaning. When an event occurs, it often triggers a belief (B) or thought about what happened. This thought might be accurate or it might be a distorted or inaccurate reflection of reality. The consequences (C) of the thought is the triggering of feelings and behaviors.

Teaching the A.B.C. formula is an important first step in helping students to help themselves. Cognitive shift is the key to change as the students learn to ask themselves if their thoughts are true reflections of reality, and if their thoughts are helping them reach their goals or taking them in the right direction.

It is important for students to understand that their thoughts are the catalyst for both their emotions and actions (behaviors). For example, a student may report he or she feels frustrated or inadequate. It is essential students search for and target the thought that preceded the feelings.

The success of C.B.T. hinges on one's ability to grasp that events themselves are neutral. It is one's thoughts about the event that produce either negative or positive feelings resulting in an action or inaction. Obstructive thoughts may take different forms, but are nonetheless unhelpful and distressing. For example, the anxious student might think: "This is awful. I can't bear it. This is absolutely the worst thing that could happen!" The angry and explosive student might think: "This is so unfair. She can't treat me this way. I will show her that she can't control me." The sad student might think: "What's the point? I will probably fail anyway. Everyone is right, I am useless." A person's behavior also creates an impression on others that, in turn, may produce a reaction. Cause and effect are cyclical in that one's thoughts about an event produce feelings and behaviors. Other people notice our display of feelings and behaviors and react accordingly.

The diagram below helps illustrate unhelpful thoughts manifested in an anxious student, an angry student, and a sad student. Note that even though the thoughts vary, all three create distress.

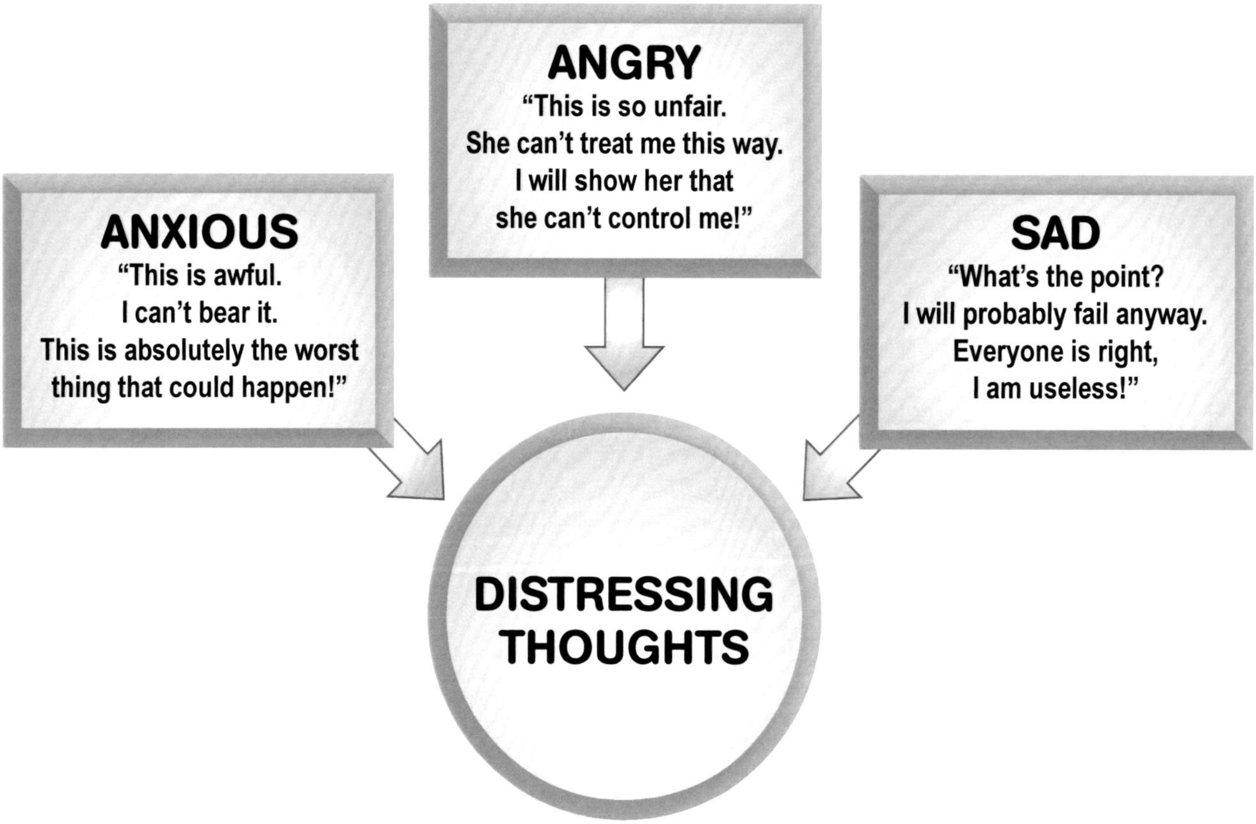

CHAPTER 4
D.E.F. Thoughts

After the students have mastered the A.B.C. steps of C.B.T., it is time to add the remainder of the steps: D.E.F. The final three steps require more Socratic-style questioning and challenge the students to actively dispute their own distorted thinking.

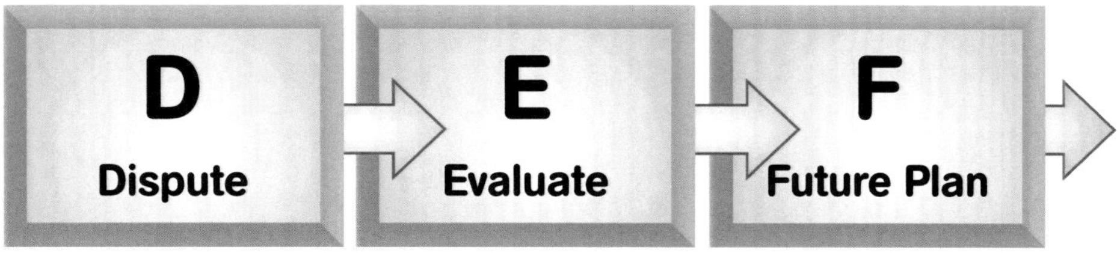

(*Note*: The questions with an asterisk (*) are on the *A.B.C.D.E.F. Worksheet*.)

Step D: Dispute

Step D requires the students to question their thoughts with a series of Socratic-style questions:

- How important is this event? *
- Is what I am thinking true? *
- What else might be going on? *
- How might this event be described in a different way? (Google Earth™ view) *
- Is there something I should do less of or more of? *
- What would others say about this situation? *

Step E: Evaluate

Step E challenges the students to carefully evaluate and scrutinize the thoughts through more Socratic questions:

- What is causing me distress? *
- Is my reaction in proportion to the event? *
- Is what I am thinking a fact or my opinion? *
- What is the evidence for it?
- What is the evidence against it?
- What is the best resolution for me? For others? For this situation? *
- Are my ideas helpful? *
- Do my plans lead me in the direction I wish to go?
- How does looking at this event from a different perspective make me feel? *

Step F: Future Plan

Step F instructs the students to create a future plan after disputing and evaluating their thoughts. This involves the skill of reframing. The distorted thought is reshaped and refitted into a more positive construct such as:

- This is a set back, but it isn't catastrophic. I can deal with it.
- I am disappointed, but I am equipped to handle this.
- Even though I prefer things were different, I am prepared to move forward.
- These feelings are temporary and will pass. I can survive this.

On the *A.B.C.D.E.F. Worksheet*, step F challenges the students to create a future plan through more Socratic questions:

- What could I do differently? *
- What strategies would be effective? *
- How could I respond to a similar situation in the future? *
- What can I focus my time and attention on to help me feel better and gain balance? *
- What things can I do to help me cope more capably when faced with a distressing event? *

After teaching all six steps, the students should be given ample opportunity to practice the goal of self-management. Students, in essence, become their own therapists. When a distressing thought occurs, the students examine their thoughts, challenge the thoughts, evaluate the thoughts, and reframe the thoughts while developing a plan for the future. Part of reframing involves developing a replacement thought. In opposition to the automatic unhelpful thought (B), the replacement thought (F) is positive and productive and devoid of feelings that create distress.

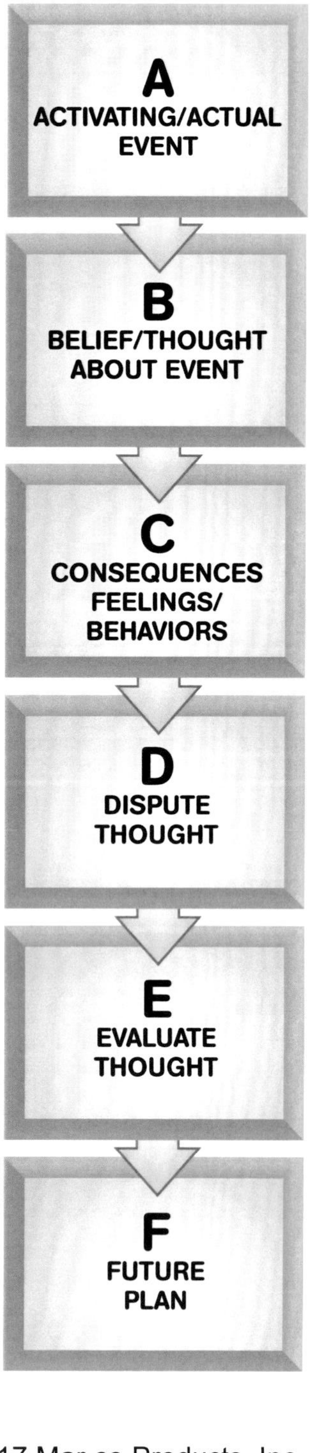

CHAPTER 5

Scaling

Scaling plays a valuable function in Cognitive Behavior Therapy. In step C, the students are asked to rate the way they feel from 1 (mild) to 5 (strong). Many medical offices use the Likert scale to assess pain levels, so the students may have some familiarity with this concept. Students will scale their feelings again at step F, after completing all of the steps (A-F). It is not expected for the students to make huge jumps on the Likert Scale. For example, if a student reports he or she is at a 1 (lowest point) he or she may be at a 2 at step F (Future Plans). Moving one point is fine in the beginning until the students become adroit at utilizing all six of the A.B.C.D.E.F. steps.

The use of Socratic questioning helps the students move along the scale. For example, you might say:

> *I noticed you are at 1. What would have to happen for you to be at 2? If you were at 2, what would I notice you doing or saying? What would others around you be doing and saying? How would I notice you responding back?*

When C.B.T. is working well for students, they will leave the room in a better frame of mind than when they came in. Over time, students will use the scale to guide themselves to a better mindset as they become more proficient at self-regulation.

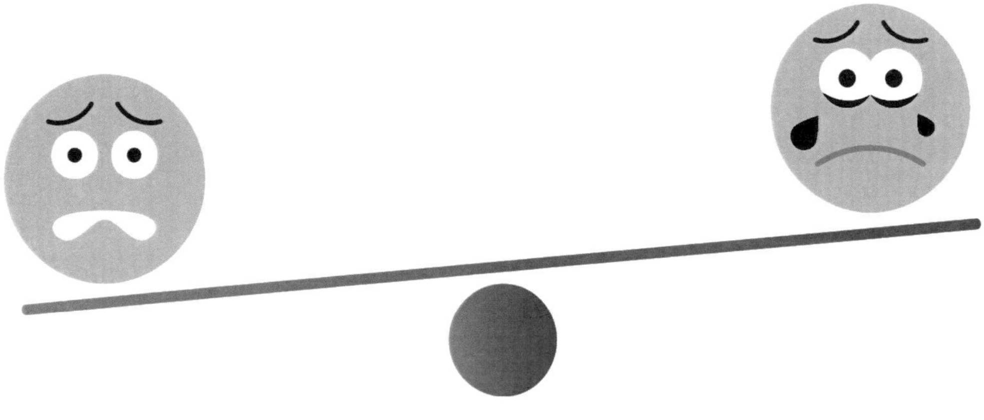

CHAPTER 6

Student Notebooks and Homework

Student Notebooks

Each student should have a notebook to keep during the duration of the sessions to contain his or her materials. Three-prong portfolios with two pocket folders work best and are inexpensive. The first page in the student notebook will be the core words page. After the core words page, the students are given five C.B.T. worksheets in sequential order to place inside their notebooks. The worksheets help the students identify their unhelpful thoughts. Once the students are able to recognize their distressing thoughts and change them, both their mindset and reactions should improve.

The order of the worksheets included in the students' notebooks is:

1. Core words (Lesson 1, pages 25-26)
2. *Thought Bubbles Worksheet* (Lesson 2, pages 27-29)
3. *Simple A.B.C. Worksheet* (Lesson 6, pages 40-41)
4. *A.B.C. Worksheet: Rethinking the Situation* (Lesson 7, pages 42-43)
5. *A.B.C.D.E.F. Worksheet 1* and *2* (Lesson 8, pages 44-47)

Student Homework

Homework takes center stage with Cognitive Behavior Therapy. Students are assigned weekly homework that is reviewed and discussed during the follow-up sessions. Worksheets are required because in order for C.B.T. to maximize its effectiveness and take root, the students need to practice these new skills. Both the counselor and the students gain insight into thought patterns and ways of reacting and responding by working through and reviewing the worksheets. The worksheets get to the heart of the students' destructive thoughts that are wrecking havoc on their emotional state. The counselor should guide the students with underlying questions such as: Does this thought, feeling, or behavior take you in the direction you want to go? or Why are you working so hard for something you don't want?

The following reproducible worksheets are given as homework assignments:

Thought Bubbles Worksheet (page 58 or PDF)
Simple A.B.C. Worksheet (page 73 or PDF)
A.B.C. Worksheet: Rethinking the Situation (page 74 or PDF)
A.B.C.D.E.F. Worksheet 1 and *2* (pages 75-76 or PDF)

CHAPTER 7

Optional Supportive Teaching Tools for C.B.T.

This program includes optional teaching tools to help the students develop self-help or self-regulation skills after being taught the A.B.C.D.E.F. steps of Cognitive Behavior Therapy. Some of the tools function as reset buttons for the students. The following optional teaching tools are for students who may need extra support in their acquirement and application of C.B.T:

- Journaling Activity
- Stand Down Card Activity
- Pleasant Times Activity
- Calm Down Card Activity

Journaling Activity (ACTIVITY INSTRUCTIONS: PAGE 48)

Journaling is a long-standing and effective way to express and release feelings. A small composition book/journal/spiral bound notebook for the students to keep and write in whenever they feel the need allows them to self soothe. Journals are private and should not be shared unless the student volunteers to do so. Small inexpensive notebooks are easily found at dollar stores. Journals can also be handmade with construction paper, tag board, and paper. Smaller journals can fit inside the pocket folders of the students' notebooks.

Stand Down Card Activity (ACTIVITY INSTRUCTIONS: PAGES 48-49 – CARD: PAGE 77)

The *Stand Down Card* (page 77 or PDF) serves as a quick reference in the form of questions. The questions help remind the students to mentally protect themselves when they are experiencing upsetting thought(s) by reshaping them, managing their feelings, and choosing appropriate actions or reactions. Students read and respond to the questions on the card. The cards should be kept in the students' notebooks or desks and/or in a place they can quickly refer to it quickly in the classroom.

Pleasant Times Activity (ACTIVITY INSTRUCTIONS: PAGE 49 – WORKSHEET: PAGE 78)

The practice of recording and scheduling pleasant activities is linked with research on gratitude. On the *Pleasant Times* worksheet (page 78 or PDF), the students list one good thing that happened and one good thing they are looking forward to. Ideally, this is done daily but can also be done weekly. The students' ideas are discussed at follow-up sessions. Setting aside time to experience enjoyable activities or people, and being thankful for this opportunity, often produces hopefulness and optimism. It is important to stress to the students that simple things (versus grandiose or elaborate plans) such as sitting under a tree or looking for a four-leaf clover can bring pleasure. The *Pleasant Times* worksheet may be kept inside the students' notebooks.

Calm Down Card Activity (ACTIVITY INSTRUCTIONS: PAGE 50 – CARD: PAGE 79)

The *Calm Down Card* (page 79 or PDF) presents strategies the students can use at school (and at home) to self-regulate their emotional state. The *Calm Down Card* lists several activities the students can do in order to better manage their emotions and behaviors. The following ideas listed on the card can help the students reset:

- Count to 10
- Go for a walk
- Visualize or go to a quiet, calm place
- Listen to music or read a book
- Draw or paint
- Write about your feelings
- Exercise! Do yoga or jump rope
- Talk it out

The cards should be kept in the students' notebooks or desks and/or in a place they can refer to them quickly in the classroom.

CHAPTER 8

Summary

Cognitive Behavior Therapy is regarded as a DIY (do it yourself) counseling approach. The goal is for the students to be able to work out their own problems once they have honed the necessary skills through repeated practice. When students are able to recognize their own destructive thoughts, and change those unhelpful thoughts through reframing, both their feelings and behaviors are transformed.

This curriculum is meant for school counselors to provide brief, short-term counseling to students in a school setting. It is not intended to be or replace therapy. Students needing more intensive work outside of school are best referred to a licensed practicing therapist.

SECTION 2

Teaching Cognitive Behavior Therapy To Students

Optional Pre-Teaching of Skill-Building Activities

Suggested Grade Levels: 3-8 **Time Frame: 30 Minutes for Each Activity**

These activities target students who need to improve the building-block skills related to C.B.T. The activities build on one another and are best done in sequential order. For best practice, teach each activity described below: *Feelings, Self-Regulation Color Wheel, Perspective, Fact or Opinion, Actions and Reactions.*

See pages 8-10 for additional information regarding each activity.

FEELINGS ACTIVITY

Materials Required:

- ☐ Picture books on the topic of feelings (see *Resources* section, page 80)
- ☐ Online video clips on the topic of feelings (see *Resources* section, page 80)
- ☐ Interactive whiteboard or white dry erase board and markers
- ☐ Simple stick puppets (optional)

Purpose:

To help the students understand the range of feelings we all experience and learn self-regulation techniques to manage those feelings when they are overwhelmed, frustrated, etc.

Activity Instructions:

1. Read picture books and/or watch Online videos on the topic of feelings with the students, then discuss the books/videos.

2. Have the students draw faces reflecting a wide range of emotions using an interactive whiteboard or a white dry erase board and markers. (For example, happy, sad, angry, worried, bored, frustrated, excited, etc.)

3. Ask students questions such as: "What makes you happy?" or " When do you feel bored?"

4. *Optional*: Have the students act out simple puppet plays where the puppets experience different emotions, explaining the reasons behind the emotions and how the characters are managing their emotions. (For example, A puppet might say: "I am feeling worried today because my grandmother is in the hospital. I am going to draw her a picture for her hospital room. Have you ever felt worried before?")

SELF-REGULATION COLOR WHEEL ACTIVITY

Materials Required:

- ☐ 2-sided copy of the *Self-Regulation Color Wheel* (front) *People, Places, Things, Activities* (back) on medium- to heavy-weight paper or card stock for each student and the leader (pages 53-54 - black and white version or PDF - color and black and white versions)
- ☐ Green, yellow, red, orange, blue, and purple marker for each student if color printing is unavailable

Purpose:

To teach the students how to identify their emotions using a color wheel and regulate themselves to a point on the color wheel where they can be productive

Activity Instructions:

1. Give each student a two-sided copy of the *Self-Regulation Color Wheel* and, if using the black and white version of the worksheet, markers to color the sections of the wheel.

2. Discuss the different colors and the fluidity and blending of colors/feelings throughout the day.

3. Have the students list people, places, and things or activities that help them achieve and maintain balance on the back of the worksheet.

4. Tell the students to place their *Self-Regulation Color Wheel*s in their student notebooks and refer to the worksheet when they need help self-regulating their emotions and behaviors.

PERSPECTIVE ACTIVITY

Materials Required:

- ☐ On computer: 3D optical illusions and/or a connection to Google Earth™

Purpose:

To help the students understand and accept that others might see things in a different perspective

Activity Instructions:

1. Ask the students to stand in three different locations in a classroom, then ask what the see.

2. Discuss how a person's perspective changes depending on his or her viewpoint, and the importance of respecting other people's viewpoints.

3. Expand the lesson on perspective by showing students 3D optical illusions and/or Google Earth images.

FACT OR OPINION ACTIVITY

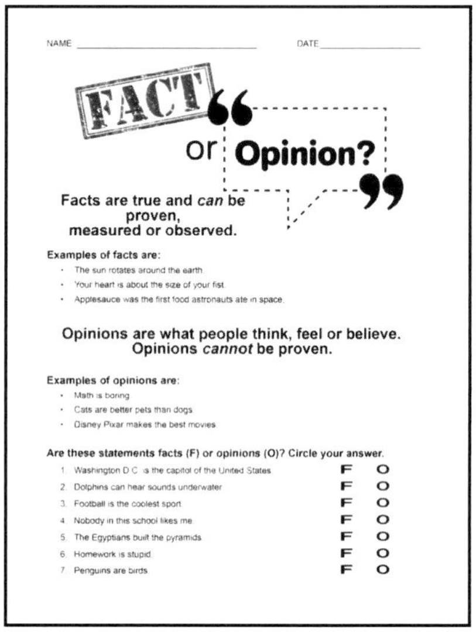
NAME DATE

FACT or Opinion?

Facts are true and *can* be proven, measured or observed.

Examples of facts are:
- The sun rotates around the earth
- Your heart is about the size of your fist.
- Applesauce was the first food astronauts ate in space.

Opinions are what people think, feel or believe. Opinions *cannot* be proven.

Examples of opinions are:
- Math is boring
- Cats are better pets than dogs
- Disney Pixar makes the best movies

Are these statements facts (F) or opinions (O)? Circle your answer.

1. Washington D.C. is the capitol of the United States F O
2. Dolphins can hear sounds underwater F O
3. Football is the coolest sport F O
4. Nobody in this school likes me F O
5. The Egyptians built the pyramids F O
6. Homework is stupid F O
7. Penguins are birds F O

Materials Required:

- ☐ *Fact or Opinion?* worksheet for each student and the leader (page 55 or PDF)
- ☐ Interactive whiteboard or white dry erase board and markers

Purpose:

To help the students understand the difference between facts and opinions

Activity Instructions:

1. Give each student a copy of the *Fact or Opinion?* worksheet.
2. Discuss with the students what makes a statement a fact and what makes it an opinion. Include suggestions that reflect faulty thinking—assuming or believing an opinion is a fact. (For example, "Everyone thinks I'm' stupid." or "My teacher is mean.") Emphasize that in C.B.T. unhelpful thoughts are evaluated to determine if the thoughts are facts or opinions.
3. Make two columns on the interactive whiteboard or dry erase board. Label one column *Facts* and the other *Opinions*. Have students list what they believe are facts and opinions on the board.

ACTIONS AND REACTIONS ACTIVITY

Materials Required:

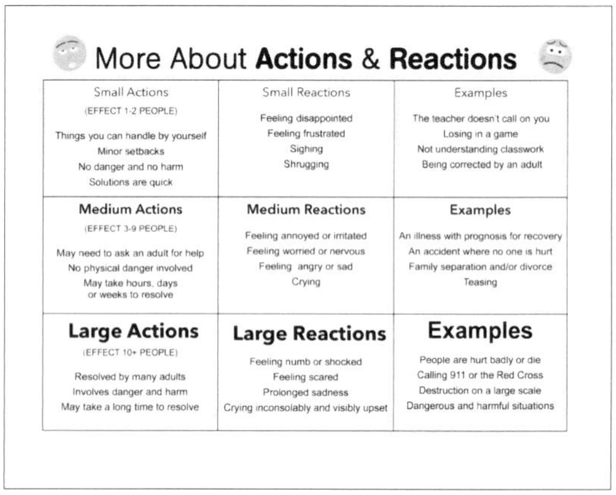
More About **Actions** & **Reactions**

Small Actions (EFFECT 1-2 PEOPLE)	Small Reactions	Examples
Things you can handle by yourself Minor setbacks No danger and no harm Solutions are quick	Feeling disappointed Feeling frustrated Sighing Shrugging	The teacher doesn't call on you Losing in a game Not understanding classwork Being corrected by an adult
Medium Actions (EFFECT 3-9 PEOPLE)	**Medium Reactions**	**Examples**
May need to ask an adult for help No physical danger involved May take hours, days or weeks to resolve	Feeling annoyed or irritated Feeling worried or nervous Feeling angry or sad Crying	An illness with prognosis for recovery An accident where no one is hurt Family separation and/or divorce Teasing
Large Actions (EFFECT 10+ PEOPLE)	**Large Reactions**	**Examples**
Resolved by many adults Involves danger and harm May take a long time to resolve	Feeling numb or shocked Feeling scared Prolonged sadness Crying inconsolably and visibly upset	People are hurt badly or die Calling 911 or the Red Cross Destruction on a large scale Dangerous and harmful situations

- ☐ *Actions and Reactions* and *More About Actions and Reactions* worksheets for each student and the leader (pages 56 and 57 or PDF)
- ☐ Interactive whiteboard or white dry erase board and markers

Purpose:

To teach the students that the size of a reaction should be proportionate the size of the action

Activity Instructions:

1. Give each student a copy of *Actions and Reactions* and *More About Actions and Reactions*.
2. Discuss the two worksheets with the students.

LESSON 1

Core Words

Suggested Grade Levels: 3-8

Time Frame: 30-45 Minutes

Materials Required:

For each student:

- ☐ Student notebook: Three-prong portfolio with two pocket folders
- ☐ *Pre- and Post-Test* (page 52 or PDF)
- ☐ Paper and pencil
- ☐ Drawing paper and markers

  or
- ☐ Computers/Tablets with Internet access to a "word cloud" program such as: Wordle™ (wordle.net) or Word it Out™ (worditout.com)

Purpose:

To guide the students in accepting that what they value and believe is important

Pre-Lesson Preparation:

Gather the necessary materials.

Print/copy one copy of the *Pre- and Post-Test* for each student.

If you are using computers/tablets, review how to use the chosen "word cloud" program.

Lesson Instructions:

Pre-Test Instructions

Give each student a copy of the *Pre- and Post-Test* and, if necessary, a pencil. Have the students complete the test. Collect the tests and save them for evaluation after the students complete the test again in Lesson 8. The test questions and answers are:

1. We have thoughts before we have feelings. (TRUE)
2. You can control your feelings by focusing on your thoughts. (TRUE)
3. I am familiar with and can name all 11 of the C.B.T. animal characters. (TRUE)
4. In the A.B.C. model of C.B.T., B stands for behavior. (FALSE)

5. The Insidious Shadow represents the unknown or the "what ifs" of life. (TRUE)
6. A dogmatic thought creates anxiety, and is persistent and reoccurring. (TRUE)
7. Steps D and E of the A.B.C.D.E.F. model of C.B.T. involve questioning and scrutinizing one's distressing thoughts. (TRUE)
8. Scaling, in C.B.T., means how much you weigh. (FALSE)
9. Our emotions produce physical sensations. (TRUE)
10. I know many ways to regulate my feelings and behaviors, and how to change and rethink my unhelpful thoughts. (TRUE)

Core Words Activity Overview

While not a component of Cognitive Behavior Therapy, the core words activity can easily be incorporated into the C.B.T. framework. Research suggests that having students write down their thoughts and core beliefs helps to build and sustain resiliency.

Core Words Activity Instructions

1. Give each a student a notebook and a piece of paper. Have the students write their spontaneous thoughts about what they value and hold dear.

2. After writing their spontaneous thought, tell the students to list the essence of their beliefs in one or two words. They should write (or type) what defines them and/or what they value. What things have deep meaning to them? There are no set limits on how many core words the students can have.

3. Have the students transform their core words into graphics. (The graphics can be generated through a free Online word cloud program such as Wordle™ (wordle.net) or Word it Out™ (worditout.com) or drawn on paper using markers.

4. The completed core graphics will be used as the first page of each student's notebook, which is explained in detail on page 16.

5. Remind the students to bring their notebooks to the next session.

Conclusion:

Conclude the lesson by saying:

In this session, we examined our foundation or our inner core. The words you selected represent those things to which you attach value and importance.

LESSON 2
Recording and Understanding Thoughts

Suggested Grade Levels: 3-8

Time Frame: 30-45 Minutes

Materials Required:

For the leader:

- ☐ *Thought Bubbles Worksheet* (page 58 or PDF)
- ☐ *The Girl with Negative Thoughts* or a similar picture (page 59 or PDF)
- ☐ Computer or Interactive whiteboard to display PDFs of the worksheets (optional)

For each student:

- ☐ 3 copies of the *Thought Bubbles Worksheet* (page 58 or PDF)
- ☐ Student notebook

Purpose:

To help the students understand the connection between thoughts, feelings, and behaviors

Pre-Lesson Preparation:

Print/copy one copy of the *Thought Bubbles Worksheet* for the leader and three copies for each student. *Optional*: have the PDF of the worksheet ready to display on a computer or interactive whiteboard.

Print/copy the picture of *The Girl with Negative Thoughts* to show the students or have the PDF of the picture ready to display on a computer or interactive whiteboard.

Lesson Instructions:

Thought Bubbles Worksheet Activity Overview

Cognitive Behavior Therapy focuses on thoughts with an almost surgical precision. Thoughts are the basis of feelings and actions. Events themselves are neutral, but our thoughts or interpretations about these events are laden and powerful. This might be a new concept to some who are accustomed to stating their feelings to justify action or inaction. Considerable care and attention is given to helping the students discover the thoughts they have before their feeling(s) develop. Thoughts are the precursors to feelings and behaviors. In C.B.T., the most important battle is the battlefield of the mind.

The *Thought Bubbles Worksheets* are required homework in C.B.T. Students complete the worksheet when they become upset or distressed. The *Thought Bubbles Worksheet* aids both the counselor and the students in identifying and targeting thoughts that are producing and maintaining the feelings. This assignment correlates with step B (belief and/or thought about the activating event) in the A.B.C. formula for C.B.T. The completed *Thought Bubbles Worksheets* are discussed at the next session.

Once the students can successfully complete the *Thought Bubbles Worksheet*, they will be discontinued and replaced with the following worksheets in sequential order:

1. *Simple A.B.C. Worksheet* (page 73 or PDF)
2. *A.B.C. Worksheet: Rethinking the Situation* (page 74 or PDF)
3. *A.B.C.D.E.F. Worksheet 1* and *2* (pages 75-76 or PDF)

Thought Bubbles Worksheet Activity Instructions

1. Give each student three copies of the *Thought Bubbles Worksheet*. Make sure each student has brought his/her notebook to the session.

2. Show the *Thought Bubbles Worksheet* to the students. The format of the worksheet is:

   When (BRIEF DESCRIPTION OF THE EVENT/SITUATION), I thought ...

3. The worksheet is explained verbally, and the students follow along. (*Note*: The students will complete the worksheets in writing as homework, see #5, page 29.) Demonstrate and explain how to fill in the worksheet as you read aloud and discuss the following situations:

   SITUATION 1

   A.J. becomes increasingly agitated in math class. He repeatedly calls out loud: "Why do we have to do this stuff anyway? Man, I hate math." After the teacher asks A.J. to quiet down, he pushes his math book to the floor and walks out of the classroom. In the office, A.J. reports that the teacher made him mad.

   Ask the students: *What thoughts might have been running through A.J.'s head when he first saw the math assignment?* (For example, " I don't know how to do any of this." "How am I supposed to know this stuff?" "This is stupid. I hate my teacher. I'm out of here!")

   SITUATION 2

   Casey is a good student and always receives high marks on her class assignments and report cards. Last year, while taking a state end-of-the-year exam, Casey felt physically sick. She failed the exam. Now, whenever Casey thinks about this year's state exam, she gets a stomachache and fears she will vomit at school. Casey is also worried she will fail the state exam again and have to repeat the grade.

   Ask the students: *What thoughts might have been running through Casey's head as she thought about the upcoming exam?* (For example, "My stomach hurts. Oh, no! I think I'm going to be sick." "Please don't let me throw up and gross everyone out!" I don't want to repeat this grade!" "What if I get sick again and fail the exam?")

4. To encourage discussion, ask the students the following questions:

   What feelings might result from A.J. and Casey's thoughts?
   How might A.J. and Casey behave?
   What physical symptoms might they experience?
   How might other kids or adults react to the way A.J. and Casey behaved?
   How might A.J. and Casey react to the other students' reactions?

5. Make sure each student understands how to complete the *Thought Bubbles Worksheet* before giving the following homework assignment. Say:

   There are four thought bubbles on each Thought Bubbles Worksheet. *You don't have to fill in all four thought bubbles, but you must complete at least one thought bubble on each sheet. Complete the three worksheets before our next session on (DATE).* (*Note*: If you meet with students weekly, this means the students will complete three worksheets during the week. Recording thoughts is a critical step in the C.B.T. process.)

6. Tell the student to put their *Thought Bubbles Worksheets* in their notebooks.

Negative Thoughts Activity Overview

An effective visual to highlight to students how thoughts affect us can be achieved with *The Girl with Negative Thoughts* picture. The picture shows a young girl surrounded by self-disparaging statements that represent her unhelpful thoughts about herself.

Negative Thoughts Activity Instructions

1. Show *The Girl with Negative Thoughts* or a similar picture to the students. (Similar pictures can be created by writing words or comments onto a picture using the text box feature of Microsoft™ Word.

2. Emphasize that the picture sends a powerful message about how our thoughts impact both our feelings and behaviors.

3. To generate discussion, ask the students the following questions:

   What kinds of feelings might negative thoughts stir up?
   What kind of reactions or inactions might result from negative thoughts?
   Are negative thoughts discouraging or encouraging?
   What could be some of the consequences of negative thoughts?

4. Remind the students to bring their notebooks to the next session.

Conclusion:

Conclude the lesson by saying:

In this session, we talked about how our thoughts greatly impact our emotions, and how our emotions impact our behavior. By altering unhelpful or negative thoughts, we can change how we react to difficult or challenging situations.

LESSON 3

The Characters of C.B.T. – Part 1

Suggested Grade Levels: 3-8 **Time Frame: 30-45 Minutes**

Materials Required:

For the leader:

- ☐ *C.B.T. Animal Characters Mini-Posters* (pages 60-70 or PDF)
- ☐ C.B.T. animal character descriptions (pages 31-32 or PDF)
- ☐ *C.B.T. Animal Characters Posters* (optional - download only)
- ☐ Computer or interactive whiteboard to display PDFs of the posters (optional)

For each student:

- ☐ Student notebook (*Note:* The notebooks are not used in this session, but it may be helpful for the students to have them on hand if a question from a previous lesson needs to be addressed.)

Purpose:

To help the students identify self-defeating thoughts by associating those thoughts with cartoon animal characters

Pre-Lesson Preparation:

Print/copy the *C.B.T. Animal Characters Mini-Posters* to show the students or have the PDFs of the characters ready to display on a computer or interactive whiteboard.

Print/copy the C.B.T. animal character descriptions for the leader.

Optional: Print the *C.B.T. Animal Characters Posters* to display in the classroom (The posters are designed to be printed in color on 11" x 17" medium- to heavy-weight paper. They can be printed in grayscale and/or on smaller-sized sheets by choosing the *reduce to fit* setting on your printer.)

Lesson Instructions:

Homework Review

Discuss the students' *Thought Bubbles Worksheets* assigned as homework in Lesson 2.

C.B.T. Animal Characters Activity Overview

Beck identified several automatic obstructive thoughts in his Cognitive Behavior Therapy. These thoughts are reoccurring and play continually through the mind effectively blocking hope and change.

The A.B.C.s of C.B.T. presents 11 cartoon animal characters that are used as visual references to identify forms of destructive thinking. In this lesson, all 11 animal characters are briefly introduced, then five of the C.B.T. animal characters are discussed in more detail. All five characters should be introduced, but if the students identify more with some of the characters, it is fine to emphasize those which resonate the strongest with the group. The goal is for the students to have a clear understanding of the animal characters and what self-defeating thoughts each character represents. In the next lesson, six additional C.B.T. animal characters will be introduced.

C.B.T. Animal Characters Activity Instructions

1. Introduce each of the C.B.T. animal characters to the students by showing them the picture of the animal and saying only the name of the character (For example, Single-Minded Skunk or Filtering Flamingo).

2. Discuss the following five C.B.T. animal characters in more detail:

    <u>SINGLE-MINDED SKUNK</u> (PAGE 60)

    Single-Minded Skunk sees things in **BLACK** and **WHITE** with nothing in the middle. Things fall neatly into two categories: good or bad, right or wrong. This rigid thinking is inflexible and ignores or denies gradients such as gray areas or mitigating factors.

    <u>GENERAL OSTRICH</u> (PAGE 61)

    General Ostrich is quick to make sweeping statements and oversimplify things. Large categories are covered with pronouns such as everyone or nobody. Common adverbs used by General Ostrich include always, never, every time. If there are exceptions, General Ostrich **STICKS HIS HEAD IN THE SAND** and either ignores or refuses to acknowledge them.

    <u>FILTERING FLAMINGO</u> (PAGE 62)

    Filtering Flamingo wears eye**SHADES** so that everything she sees is shaded and filtered. Events are run through a sieve with only certain items remaining. Flamingo sifts around ignoring some evidence while overemphasizing other evidence. Filtering Flamingo carefully picks out of the strainer and pays attention to a particular type of evidence and ignores the rest.

    <u>COUNT BATULA</u> (PAGE 63)

Count Batula disregards the positive and exaggerates the negative. **RIGHT OFF THE BAT,** he quickly qualifies any compliment with statements such as "You have to like me you're my teacher." or "You're my mom, so your supposed to say things like that." If something goes his way, he deduces it was a fluke.

LEAP FROG (PAGE 64)

Leap Frog lives life on the edge. She **JUMPS** to conclusions and makes predications about the future based on a single occurrence. For Leap Frog, causation is pre-determined and cannot be changed. She also believes she can read people's minds and knows what they are thinking even before they know themselves.

3. *Optional*: Display the *C.B.T. Animal Characters Posters* in the room as a reminder of the lesson.

4. Remind the students to bring their notebooks to the next session.

Conclusion:

Conclude the lesson by saying:

Today, you were introduced to five C.B.T. animal characters. Be aware of any distressing thoughts that pop into your head, and think about which of the animals characters might have similar thoughts.

LESSON 4

The Characters of C.B.T. – Part 2

Suggested Grade Levels: 3-8 **Time Frame: 30-45 Minutes**

Materials Required:

For the leader:

- ☐ *C.B.T. Animal Characters Mini-Posters* (from Lesson 3)
- ☐ *C.B.T.* animal character descriptions (from Lesson 3)
- ☐ *C.B.T. Animal Characters Posters* (from Lesson 3)
- ☐ Computer or interactive whiteboard to display PDFs of the worksheets or posters (optional)

For each student:

- ☐ Student notebook (*Note:* The notebooks are not used in this session, but it may be helpful for the students to have them on hand if a question from a previous lesson needs to be addressed.)

Purpose:

To help the students identify self-defeating thoughts by associating those thoughts with animal characters

Pre-Lesson Preparation:

Gather the materials used in Lesson 3.

Lesson Instructions:

C.B.T. Characters Activity Overview

In this lesson, six new C.B.T. animal characters are presented. At the end of this lesson, the students should be able to clearly identify all eleven characters and the self-defeating thoughts associated with each one. As in the previous lesson, if the students make a stronger connection with specific characters, feature these characters in your discussions.

C.B.T. Animals Characters Activity Instructions

1. Show each of the *C.B.T. Animal Characters Mini-Posters* presented in Lesson 3. Briefly review each character's associated traits.

2. Show each of the following *C.B.T. Animal Characters Mini-Posters.* Discuss the following six characters in more detail:

   <u>LABELING LEOPARD</u> (PAGE 65)

   Labeling Leopard believes everything has its **SPOT**, and neatly labels everyone and everything. Once assigned a label, the labels are rarely changed. Things are neatly put into labeled boxes and sealed. Labels are affixed and almost always permanent.

   <u>CATASTROPHE CAT</u> (PAGE 66)

   A routine set back becomes a **CAT**astrophe in the mind of **CAT**astrophe Cat. A fairly routine obstacle becomes insurmountable and assumes epic proportions. **CAT**astrophe Cat immediately thinks of the worst possible scenario. Most events, from the minor to the major, are met with overreactions.

   <u>BADGERING BADGER AND SHOULD SHARK</u> (PAGE 67-68, PRESENTED TOGETHER)

   This particular thought pattern, plagued by shouldizing and musterbation, takes two different forms and thus has two characters. The character choice depends on the individual experiencing the often-repeated critical words such as should, must, have to, or ought to. **BAGERING** Badger epitomizes constant **NAGGING** while the treacherous **SHOULD** Shark embodies bold inflexibility. Both characters have a way of making one feel guilty, frustrated, and inadequate. Badgering Badger and Should Shark keep us locked into expectations and the fear that we will disappoint others.

   <u>FAIRNESS FALCON</u> (PAGE 69)

   Fairness Falcon is obsessed with the fairness in life and becomes visibly upset with any instance of impartiality. He carefully watches and judges if things are being handled in a **FAIR** and impartial manner. Fairness Falcon will accept no compromise on this issue and becomes irate when he perceives he is being treated in an inequitable manner. He takes the issue of fairness personally believing he alone is the target, which often leaves him resentful and angry.

   <u>PUFFER FISH</u> (PAGE 70)

   Puffer Fish can make herself bigger or smaller. Puffer Fish tends to either downplay or overplay events. Puffer Fish sees things way out of proportion to how they actually are. Reality is either **PUFFED UP** and exaggerated or underestimated with Puffer Fish.

3. *Optional*: Display the *C.B.T. Characters Posters* in the room as a reminder of the lesson.

4. Remind the students to bring their notebooks to the next session.

Conclusion:

Conclude the lesson by saying:

> *In this session, you were introduced to six more C.B.T. animal characters. Be aware of any distressing thoughts that pop into your head, and think about which of the animals characters might have similar thoughts.*

LESSON 5

Dogmatic Dog and The Insidious Shadow

Suggested Grade Levels: 3-8 **Time Frame: 30-45 Minutes**

Materials Required:

For the leader:

- ☐ *C.B.T. Animal Characters Mini-Posters* (from Lessons 3 and 4)
- ☐ *C.B.T. Characters Posters* (from Lessons 3 and 4)
- ☐ *Dogmatic Dog* picture (page 71 or PDF)
- ☐ *The Insidious Shadow* picture (page 72 or PDF)
- ☐ Handmade or purchased magic wand (optional)
- ☐ Computer or interactive whiteboard to display PDFs of the worksheets or posters (optional)

For each student:

- ☐ Student notebook (*Note:* The notebooks are not used in this session, but it may be helpful for the students to have them on hand if a question from a previous lesson needs to be addressed.)

Purpose:

To summarize and review the C.B.T animal characters introduced in the previous two lessons and to introduce the students to Dogmatic Dog and The Insidious Shadow.

Pre-Lesson Preparation:

Gather the mini-posters and posters used in Lessons 3 and 4.

Print/copy the *Dogmatic Dog* picture and *The Insidious Shadow* picture to show the students or have the PDFs of the characters ready to display on a computer or interactive whiteboard.

Optional: Purchase or make a simple magic wand.

Lesson Instructions:

C.B.T. Characters Activity Overview

Display all 11 of the *C.B.T. Animal Characters Mini-Posters*. At this point, the students should be able to easily identify each character and the negative/disruptive thoughts it represents.

C.B.T. Animals Characters Activity Instructions

1. Show each *C.B.T. Animal Characters Mini-Poster*. Briefly review each character's associated traits.

2. Ask the students which character(s) their own thoughts most closely mirror and their reason for their choice(s).

Dogmatic Dog Activity Overview

Central to teaching the concept of dogmatic thoughts is the students' realization that distressing thoughts rarely travel alone. Dogmatic thoughts are plural, with multiple adverse thoughts increasing in strength and creating emotional havoc. For example, with Catastrophe Cat, a fairly routine occurrence such as a rainy day produces an extreme overreaction resulting in layers of harmful thoughts. Rain becomes a severe thunderstorm that becomes a tornado and flooding that becomes the mass destruction of people and property and finally becomes death and extinction. These thoughts are dogmatic in that they "dog" or "hound" a person throughout the day, and are intrusive and disruptive, like a barking dog.

Diagram of the Ascension of Distressing Thoughts

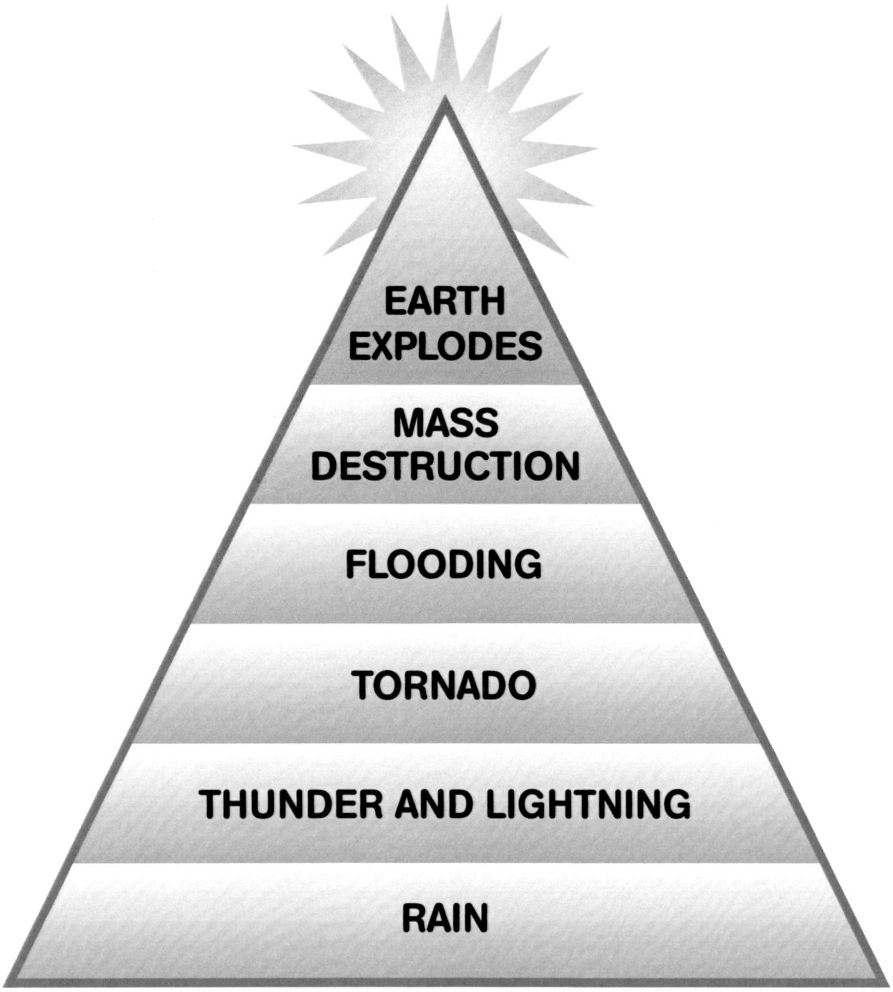

Dogmatic Dog Activity Instructions

1. Introduce the concept of *dogmatic thoughts* by asking:

   What smaller word do you see in the word dogmatic? (dog)

   Does anyone know what the word dogmatic means? (Summarize the students' answers. Give the following definition if necessary: Dogmatic means opinionated, assertive, insistent.)

2. Introduce Dogmatic Dog by saying:

   All 11 of the C.B.T. animal characters have something in common. They all have repetitive and dogmatic thoughts running continually through their minds. Although their specific thoughts might take different forms, such as in Leap Frog jumping to conclusions or General Ostrich oversimplify things, their thoughts are dogmatic in nature.

   Show the *Dogmatic Dog* picture, then continue the introduction of the character by explaining:

   <u>DOGMATIC DOG</u>

   Central to all automatic thoughts is the Dogmatic Dog character. Dogmatic Dog's thoughts are dogmatic in nature. Dogmatic thinkers believe others should share their opinions and beliefs and they have an intolerance for contradictory or conflicting beliefs. Dogmatic Dog is persistent and determined in his efforts to create emotional distress, dictate moods, and drive behaviors. Like the barking of a dog, dogmatic thoughts are intrusive and disruptive.

The Insidious Shadow Activity Overview

A byproduct of the distressing thoughts associated with the C.B.T. characters is a shadowy figure known as The Insidious Shadow. The Insidious Shadow lurks behind each anxiety-producing thought, and while not an actual C.B.T. character, The Insidious Shadow sows discontent. The Insidious Shadow represents the unknown or the ambiguous "what ifs" of life. It produces fear of the future and often immobilizes action paralyzing the individual with dread that any action might make the situation worse than it already is. In essence, the students may find themselves fighting on two fronts. The front defended by the C.B.T. characters, and an almost hidden second front guarded by The Insidious Shadow.

The Insidious Shadow picture helps the students to visualize the haunting aspects of incessant distressing thoughts that doggedly follow us wherever we go.

To better understand the concept of The Insidious Shadow, it is helpful to borrow the idea of waving a magic wand from Solution-Focused Therapy.

Solution-Focused Brief Therapy (S.F.B.T.) was developed in the late 1970s by Steve de Shazer, Insoo Kim Berg, and others at the Milwaukee Brief Family Therapy Center. S.F.B.T. focuses on solutions versus problems. Attention is on establishing clear goals and developing a plan for the present and the future. Clients are taught how to look for exceptions and to do what works. S.F.B.T. makes good use of rating or scaling ones level of feelings, as well as posing questions related to the clients coping strategies. Two of the hallmark features of S.F.B.T. are making good use of both Socratic questions and compliments. More information on S.F.B.T. can be found through the website for the Institute for Solution-Focused Therapy (solutionfocused.net) and the Solution-Focused Brief Therapy Association (sfbta.org).

By asking the students some of the trademark questions (see below) associated with Solution-Focused Therapy, they are equipped to do battle against The Insidious Shadow.

The Insidious Shadow Activity Instructions

1. Show the *The Insidious Shadow* picture to the students. Then say:

   Imagine that a miracle happened over night. During the night, a magic wand was waved over your head and your problem no longer exists. You are set free. Imagine how you might behave differently now that your problem has vanished. What will you notice or feel when you wake up without this problem? What signs will alert you that the problem has disappeared? Now that this problem has vanished, how will your life be different? How will you behave differently?

2. Ask the students to act as if the miracle has already happened. That is, to behave as if their problems suddenly vanished. Say:

   Focus on what might happen after your problem is gone. By imagining your problem is non-existent, The Insidious Shadow loses its power over you.

3. Remind the students to bring their notebooks to the next session.

Conclusion:

Conclude the lesson by saying:

Identifying and recognizing when dogmatic thoughts occur are the key to stopping them. In addition, worrying about what might or could happen creates a shadow of fear preventing you from living the life you desire.

LESSON 6

Simple A.B.C. Worksheet

Suggested Grade Levels: 3-8 **Time Frame: 30-45 Minutes**

Materials Required:

For the leader:

- ☐ *C.B.T. Animal Characters Mini-Posters* (from previous lessons)
- ☐ *C.B.T. Characters Posters* (from previous lessons)
- ☐ *Simple A.B.C. Worksheet* (page 73 or PDF)
- ☐ Computer or interactive whiteboard to display PDFs of the worksheets or posters (optional)

For each student:

- ☐ 3 copies of the *Simple A.B.C. Worksheet* (page 73 or PDF)
- ☐ Student notebook

Purpose:

To teach the students to apply the A.B.C. construct of Cognitive Behavior Therapy

Pre-Lesson Preparation:

Gather the mini-posters, pictures, and posters used in Lessons 3, 4, and 5.

Print/copy one copy of the *Simple A.B.C. Worksheet* for the leader and three copies for each student.

Lesson Instructions:

C.B.T. Animals Characters Activity Instructions

1. Display the *Dogmatic Dog* picture, *The Insidious Shadow* picture, and each of the *C.B.T. Animal Characters Mini-Posters.* Briefly review each character's associated traits.

Simple A.B.C. Worksheet Activity Overview

The *Simple A.B.C. Worksheet* is streamlined and meant to help guide the students. In the beginning, the counselor and the students work collaboratively on its completion. The aim of this joint venture is for the students to fully grasp the A.B.C. steps of C.B.T. so that in subsequent sessions and throughout their life they are able to complete the steps independently. While the students may start out using the worksheet, in time they will be able to complete the steps mentally whenever they are faced with an anxiety-producing thought (C.B.T. animal character) which becomes dogmatic in nature (Dogmatic Dog) coupled with doubts (The Insidious Shadow).

Simple A.B.C. Worksheet Activity Instructions

1. Give each student three copies of the *Simple A.B.C. Worksheet*. Make sure each student has brought his/her notebook to the session.

2. Show the *Simple A.B.C. Worksheet* to the students. The worksheet is explained verbally, and the students follow along. (*Note*: The students will complete the worksheet in writing as homework, see #5 below.) Demonstrate and explain how to fill in the worksheet as you call out typical scenarios that students face such as state exams, benchmark assessments, being unprepared in class when called on by the teacher, doing a class presentation, being corrected by a teacher publicly, etc.

3. Have the students verbally respond to each section of the worksheet so they understand the progression and connection between thoughts, feelings, and behaviors, as well as learning how to scale. (*Note:* There may be wide variance in the degree of distress these scenarios create as well as differences on how the students rate/scale the scenarios. Remain steadfast with this lesson until you are certain the students have a solid understanding of the content.)

4. Display or point to the *C.B.T. Animal Characters Mini-Posters* again, then ask the students to identify which characters are linked to the distressing thoughts they have voiced during the *Simple A.B.C. Worksheet* activity. For example, if the leader calls out "state assessments," the students may say: "I just know I'll fail. I stink at reading." (Leap Frog) or "I will be held back, and everyone in the school will know I failed and think I'm stupid." (Catastrophe Cat) or "It's not fair that only fifth graders have to take the science exam. I hate science it is so boring." (Fairness Falcon)

5. Make sure each student understands how to complete the *Simple A.B.C. Worksheet* before giving the following homework assignment. Say:

   Chose distressing events you have experienced or experience during the week and use those experiences to complete each Simple A.B.C. Worksheet *as a written homework assignment. Complete the three worksheets before our next session on (DATE).* (*Note*: If you meet with the students weekly, this means they will complete three worksheets during the week to practice the A.B.C. model.)

6. Tell the students to put their *Simple A.B.C. Worksheets* in their notebooks.

7. Remind the students to bring their notebooks to the next session.

Conclusion:

Conclude the lesson by saying:

In this lesson, we learned how to evaluate our thoughts using the A.B.C. steps of C.B.T. The letter A stands for the activating or actual event or what happened, B is the belief or thought about the event, and C is the consequences—how those thoughts make us feel, behave, and react.

LESSON 7

A.B.C. Worksheet: Rethinking the Situation

Suggested Grade Levels: 3-8 **Time Frame: 30-45 Minutes**

Materials Required:

For the leader:

- ☐ *C.B.T. Animal Characters Mini-Posters* (from previous lessons)
- ☐ *C.B.T. Characters Posters* (from previous lessons)
- ☐ *Dogmatic Dog* picture (from previous lessons)
- ☐ *The Insidious Shadow* picture (from previous lessons)
- ☐ *A.B.C. Worksheet: Rethinking the Situation* (page 74 or PDF)
- ☐ Computer or interactive whiteboard to display PDFs of the worksheets or posters (optional)

For each student:

- ☐ 3 copies of the *A.B.C. Worksheet: Rethinking the Situation* (page 74 or PDF)
- ☐ Student notebook

Purpose:

To teach the students how to rethink or reframe a distressing thought

Pre-Lesson Preparation:

Gather the mini-posters, pictures, and posters used in the previous lessons.

Print/copy one copy of the *A.B.C. Worksheet: Rethinking the Situation* for the leader and three copies for each student.

Lesson Instructions:

Homework Review

Discuss the students' *Simple A.B.C. Worksheets* assigned as homework in Lesson 6.

C.B.T. Animals Characters Activity Instructions

1. Display the *Dogmatic Dog* picture, *The Insidious Shadow* picture, and each of the *C.B.T. Animal Characters Mini-Posters.* Briefly review each character's associated traits.

A.B.C. Worksheet: Rethinking the Situation Activity Overview

After the students have practiced and understand the *Simple A.B.C. Worksheet*, the *A.B.C. Worksheet: Rethinking the Situation* is introduced. The *A.B.C. Worksheet: Rethinking the Situation* adds a middle component called *rethinking* or *reframing*. Rethinking is reframing or revising a distressing thought. This involves an approach where the anxiety-causing thoughts are examined and even challenged. The harsh thoughts are cast in a new light, a light that is softer and less anxiety producing. This involves a more advanced skill. Students will initially need guidance in order to effectively rethink their thoughts. Guidance is given in the form of Socratic questions that the leader (and later students) asks. The *A.B.C. Worksheet: Rethinking the Situation* lists some of the Socratic questioning methods traditionally associated with Cognitive Behavior Therapy. Rethinking is an essential component of C.B.T. Use the time in this session to guide the students in this process until they are proficient in this step.

A.B.C. Student Worksheet: Rethinking the Situation Activity Instructions

1. Give each student three copies of the *A.B.C. Worksheet: Rethinking the Situation*. Make sure each student has brought his/her notebook to the session.

2. Show the *A.B.C. Worksheet: Rethinking the Situation* to the students. The worksheet is explained verbally, and the students follow along. (*Note*: The students will complete the worksheet in writing as homework, see #5 below.)

3. Discuss how to complete the worksheet by presenting common problems that students face in school such as needing help on an assignment, a friend who has started to act distant, receiving a low grade on a project, not being selected for a solo in the school chorus, etc.

4. Have the students verbally respond to each section of the worksheet so they understand the progression and connection between thoughts, feelings, and behaviors, as well as learning how to reframe or rethink their thoughts about the event or situation.

5. Make sure each student understands how to complete the *A.B.C. Worksheet: Rethinking the Situation* before giving the following homework assignment. Say:

   Chose distressing events you have experienced or experience during the week and use those experiences to complete each A.B.C. Worksheet: Rethinking the Situation *as a written homework assignment. Complete all three worksheets before our next session on (DATE).* (*Note*: If you meet with the students weekly, this means they will complete three worksheets during the week to practice the A.B.C. model with rethinking.)

6. Tell the student to put their *A.B.C. Worksheet: Rethinking the Situation* in their notebooks.

7. Remind the students to bring their notebooks to the next session.

Conclusion:

Conclude the lesson by saying:

Today, we learned how to change a distressing thought into a more productive thought through the process of rethinking. When negative thoughts are cast in a new light, they become less distressing and less stressful.

LESSON 8

A.B.C.D.E.F. Worksheet

Suggested Grade Levels: 3-8 **Time Frame: 30-45 Minutes**

Materials Required:

For the leader:

- ☐ *C.B.T. Animal Characters Mini-Posters* (from previous lessons)
- ☐ *C.B.T. Characters Posters* (from previous lessons)
- ☐ *Dogmatic Dog* picture (from previous lessons)
- ☐ *The Insidious Shadow* picture (from previous lessons)
- ☐ *A.B.C.D.E.F. Worksheet 1* (page 75 or PDF)
- ☐ Computer or interactive whiteboard to display PDFs of the worksheets or posters (optional)

For each student:

- ☐ *A.B.C.D.E.F. Worksheet 1* (page 75 or PDF)
- ☐ 3 copies of the *A.B.C.D.E.F. Worksheet 2* (page 76 or PDF)
- ☐ *Pre- and Post-Test* (page 52 or PDF)
- ☐ Pencil
- ☐ Student notebook

Purpose:

To teach the students all five components (A.B.C.D.E.F.) of the student worksheet

Pre-Lesson Preparation:

Gather the mini-posters, pictures, and posters used in the previous lessons.

Print/copy one copy of the *A.B.C.D.E.F. Worksheet 1* for the leader and each student.

Print/copy three copies of the *A.B.C.D.E.F. Worksheet 2* for each student.

Print/copy one copy of the *Pre- and Post-Test* for each student.

Lesson Instructions:

Homework Review

Discuss the students' *A.B.C. Worksheet: Rethinking the Situations* assigned as homework in Lesson 7.

C.B.T. Animals Characters Activity Instructions

1. Display the *Dogmatic Dog* picture, *The Insidious Shadow* picture, and each of the *C.B.T. Animal Characters Mini-Posters.* Briefly review each character's associated traits.

A.B.C.D.E.F. Worksheet Activity Overview

The *A.B.C.D.E.F. Worksheet* is introduced once the students have thoroughly mastered the *Simple A.B.C. Worksheet* and the *A.B.C. Worksheet: Rethinking the Situation*. With the addition of the D.E.F. steps to the previously learned A.B.C. steps, the students will have the necessary tools they need to not only recognize and evaluate destructive thoughts and their consequences, they will also learn to dispute (challenge), evaluate the evidence (weigh the pluses and minuses), and chart future plans (new pathways for reacting and responding).

In the D.E.F. steps of C.B.T, step D requires the students to practice disputing their distressing thoughts. Step D mandates action by not passively accepting and amplifying vexing thoughts. This process is closely related to rethinking, and the students who are effective in rethinking or reframing their distressing thoughts will easily learn this step. The ability to challenge distressing thoughts is crucial in order for the students to be able to help themselves.

At step E, the evidence is evaluated and scrutinized. Like scientists, the students learn to examine the evidence for and evidence against their angst. At step F, the students plan future paths. Students begin to look towards the future and explore news ways of managing their frustrations instead of being paralyzed by distressing thoughts, which repeat over and over again in their brains.

Step F enables the students to quickly identify their upsetting thoughts and the associated *C.B.T.* animal characters, rethink their thoughts, and create a forward movement away from their inner anguish. Students revisit the scale after completing all the steps (A-F). For example, a student's automatic and original distressing thoughts (B) might be assigned a high 5 on a 1-5 Likert scale. At step D, his/her thoughts are reframed into more manageable and neutral thoughts, and at step F assigned a mid range 3 on a 1-5 scale.

With the addition of steps D.E.F., the students have learned all six steps (A.B.C.D.E.F.) of the model.

A.B.C.D.E.F. Worksheet Activity

1. Give each student one copy of *A.B.C.D.E.F. Worksheet 1* and three copies of *A.B.C.D.E.F. Worksheet 2.* Make sure each student has brought his/her notebook to the session.

2. Show *A.B.C.D.E.F. Worksheet 1* to the students. The worksheet is explained verbally, and the students follow along. (*Note*: The students will complete the worksheet in writing as homework, see #4 page 47.)

3. Students verbally respond to each section of the worksheet. Help the students to understand the process for completing the worksheet by presenting a series of Socratic questions. The questions are derived from Cognitive Behavior Therapy and help the students clarify the A.B.C.D.E.F. steps. Call out various problematic situations students face and have them complete the *A.B.C.D.E.F. Worksheet 1* out loud. Some examples include being assigned to work with a partner on a project that you dislike, the entire class is punished for the behavior of two students, a parent signed you up for a sport in which you have no interest, missing out on a Friday school-wide activity due to a lost assignment, etc.

   Version 1 of the worksheet lists the Socratic questions and version 2 of the worksheet does not show the Socratic questions. Once the students have mastered the A.B.C.D.E.F. formula, they are able to internalize the Socratic questions and only need to refer to the headers and/or images on the worksheet to help guide them through the process. Students should leave this session with a clear understanding of how to complete the worksheet on their own.

Use the following Socratic questions to guide the students as they verbally complete *A.B.C.D.E.F. Worksheet 1*. The questions marked with an asterisk (*) can also be found on the worksheet.

Step A: Activating (Actual) Event: Who? What? When? Where?

- What happened? Give details.*

Step B: Belief/Thought: What Were You Thinking?

- What thoughts or images popped into your head? *
- Did you find these thoughts or images upsetting?
- What "buttons" did this event push?
- What meaning did you attach to your thoughts? *

Step C: Consequences: How Did You Feel? How Did You React?

- What emotions did you experience? *
- Rate your feelings from 1 (mild) to 5 (strong). *
- How did you behave? *
- What physical sensations did you experience? *
- Where did you feel the sensations in your body? *

Step D: Dispute: Question Your Thoughts

- How important is this event? *
- Is what you are thinking true? *
- What else might be going on? *
- How might this event be described in a different way? (Google Earth view) *
- Is there something you should do less of or more of? *
- Will you feel the same in three months? In six months?
- What would others say about this situation? *
- What advice would you give a friend if he or she was in a similar situation?

Step E: Evaluate: Scrutinize Your Thoughts

- What is causing your distress? *
- Is your reaction in proportion to the event? *
- Is what you are thinking a fact or your opinion? *
- What is the evidence for it?
- What is the evidence against it?
- What is the best resolution for you? For others? For this situation? *
- Are your ideas helpful? *
- Do your plans lead you in the direction you wish to go?
- How does looking at this event from a different perspective make you feel? *

Step F: Future Plans: Do What Works!

- What could you do differently? *
- What strategies would be effective? *
- How could you respond to a similar situation in the future? *
- What can you focus your time and attention on to help you feel better and gain balance? *
- What things can you do to help you cope more capably when faced with a distressing event? *

4. Make sure each student understands how to complete the *A.B.C.D.E.F. Worksheet 2* before giving the following homework assignment. Say:

   Chose distressing events you have experienced or experience during the week and use those experiences to complete each A.B.C.D.E.F. Worksheet 2 *as a written homework assignment. Complete all three worksheets before our next session on (<u>DATE</u>).* (*Note*: If you meet with the students weekly, this means they will complete three worksheets during the week to practice the A.B.C.D.E.F. model.)

5. Tell the student to put their *A.B.C.D.E.F. Worksheets* in their notebooks.

Post-Test Instructions

Give each student a copy of the *Pre- and Post-Test* and, if necessary, a pencil. Have the students complete the test. Collect the tests and compare each student's answers to those he or she gave in the pre-test. The test questions and answers can be found on pages 25-26.

Conclusion:

Thank the students for participating in the sessions, then conclude the lesson by saying:

Today, we learned to carefully examine our thoughts, challenge and evaluate those thoughts, and plan more helpful strategies to use now and in the future.

Optional Supportive Teaching Tools for C.B.T.

Suggested Grade Levels: 3-8 **Time Frame: 30-45 Minutes Each**

These four optional activities are for students needing additional support in practicing the principles of C.B.T. See pages 17-18 for additional information regarding each activity.

JOURNALING ACTIVITY (THIS ACTIVITY TAKES ABOUT10 MINUTES PER ENTRY)

Materials Required:

- ☐ Journals (small composition books or handmade journals)
- ☐ Student notebooks

Purpose:

To help the students develop strategies that give them a sense of calm when they experience distress

Activity Instructions:

1. Give each student a journal.

2. Explain to the students that the journals are for recording their private thoughts and feelings. (*Note:* By regularly writing their thoughts, the students can gain insight into their behaviors and feelings. Journaling can be used for problem-solving, reducing anxiety and stress, and building self-esteem. Journals are private and should not be shared unless the student volunteers to do so.)

3. This can be a daily homework assignment.

4. Tell the students keep their journals in their notebooks or in a spot where they can easily access them.

STAND DOWN CARD ACTIVITY

Materials Required:

- ☐ *Stand Down Card* copied/printed on medium- to heavy-weight paper for each student (page 77 or PDF)
- ☐ Student notebooks

Purpose:

To provide the students with a quick list of questions to help them reset when they are feeling upset

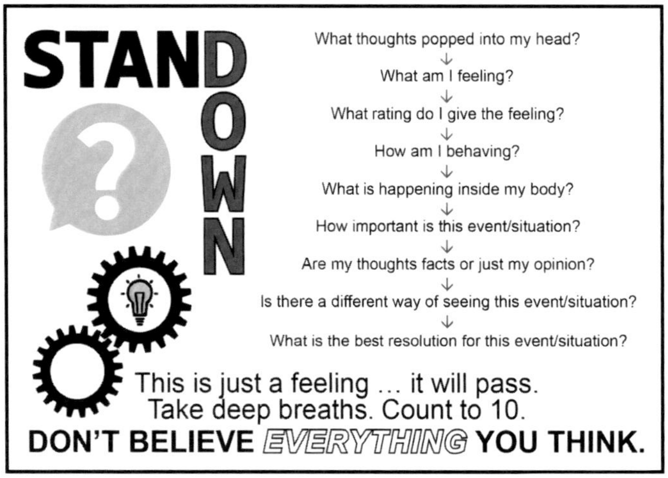

Activity Instructions:

1. Give each student a *Stand Down Card.*
2. Read the card aloud and review the questions with the students.
3. Have the students practice using the card.
4. Tell the students keep the cards in their notebooks or in a spot where they can easily access them.

PLEASANT TIMES ACTIVITY

Materials Required:

- ☐ *Pleasant Times* worksheet for each student (page 78 or PDF)
- ☐ Student notebooks

Purpose:

To help the students focus on the positive aspects of their day and build gratitude and optimism

Activity Instructions:

1. Give each student a copy of the *Pleasant Times* worksheet.
2. Point out the two columns on the worksheet. Explain to the students that in one column they should write about one good that happened to them. In the other column, they should write about something they are looking forward to.
3. This can be a homework assignment. Students can share their ideas with one another in future sessions.
4. Tell the students keep their worksheets in their notebooks

CALM DOWN CARD ACTIVITY

Materials Required:

- ☐ *Calm Down Card* copied/printed on medium- to heavy-weight paper for each student (page 79 or PDF)
- ☐ Student notebooks

Purpose:

To provide the students with a quick list of calming tools they can use to help them self-regulate

Activity Instructions:

1. Give each student a *Calm Down Card.*
2. Read the card aloud and review the strategies with the students.
3. Have the students practice using the strategies printed on the card.
4. Tell the students keep the cards in their notebooks or in a spot where they can easily access them.

SECTION 3

Reproducible Mini Posters and Worksheets

NAME ________________________________ DATE ____________________

The A.B.C.s of C.B.T.

PRE- and POST-TEST

CIRCLE YOUR ANSWER	TRUE	FALSE
1. We have thoughts before we have feelings.	T	F
2. You can control your feelings by focusing on your thoughts.	T	F
3. I am familiar with and can name all 11 of the C.B.T. animal characters.	T	F
4. In the A.B.C. model of C.B.T., B stands for behavior.	T	F
5. The Insidious Shadow represents the unknown or the "what ifs" of life.	T	F
6. A dogmatic thought creates anxiety and is persistent and reoccurring.	T	F
7. Steps D and E of the A.B.C.D.E.F. model of C.B.T. involve questioning and scrutinizing one's distressing thoughts.	T	F
8. Scaling, in C.B.T., means how much you weigh.	T	F
9. Our emotions produce physical sensations.	T	F
10. I know many ways to regulate my feelings and behaviors and how to change and rethink my unhelpful thoughts.	T	F

NAME ______________________________ DATE ____________________

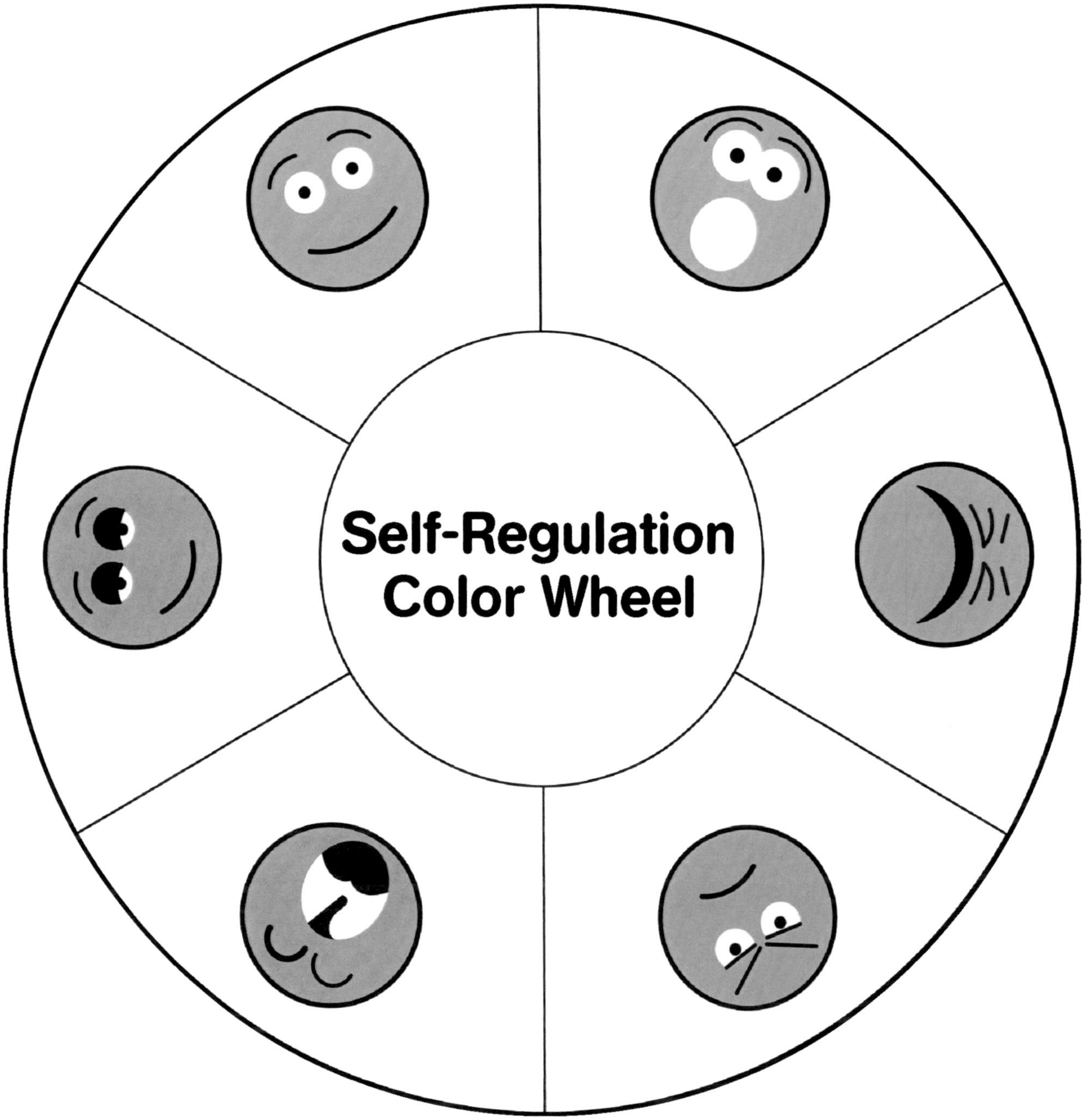

◯ **PURPLE** = listless, no energy, lazy, lethargic, slow

◯ **BLUE** = passive, relaxed, dreamy

◯ **GREEN** = balance, calm, ready to learn

◯ **YELLOW** = high energy, excited, agitated or restless, alert

◯ **ORANGE** = heightened state, revved up, frustrated

◯ **RED** = tense, charged up, strong surge of emotion, anger

List people, places, and things or activities
that help you create a balanced life …
to be calm, grounded, and motivated.

PEOPLE	PLACES	THINGS/ ACTIVITIES

NAME ________________________________ DATE ____________________

FACT or "Opinion?"

Facts are true and *can* be proven, measured or observed.

Examples of facts are:

- The earth rotates around the sun.
- Your heart is about the size of your fist.
- Applesauce was the first food astronauts ate in space.

Opinions are what people think, feel, or believe. Opinions *cannot* be proven.

Examples of opinions are:

- Math is boring.
- Cats make better pets than dogs.
- Disney Pixar makes the best movies.

Are these statements facts (F) or opinions (O)? Circle your answer.

1. Washington D.C. is the capitol of the United States.	F	O
2. Dolphins can hear sounds underwater.	F	O
3. Football is the coolest sport.	F	O
4. Nobody in this school likes me.	F	O
5. The Egyptians built the pyramids.	F	O
6. Homework is stupid.	F	O
7. Penguins are birds.	F	O

NAME ____________________ DATE ____________

Actions and Reactions

Small Actions 	Teacher not calling on you Losing in a game Forgetting homework Not understanding class work Adult reprimanding you	Feeling disappointed Feeling frustrated Sighing Shrugging
Medium Actions 	Illness An accident where no one is hurt Family separation and/or divorce Hospital stay Teasing	Feeling annoyed or irritated Feeling worried or nervous Feeling angry or sad Crying
Large Actions 	People are badly hurt Calling 911 or Red Cross Destruction and damage on a large scale Dangerous and harmful situation Death	Feeling numb or shocked Feeling scared Prolonged sadness Crying inconsolably and visibly upset

NAME ____________________ DATE ____________

More About **Actions** and **Reactions**

Small Actions (EFFECT 1-2 PEOPLE) Things you can handle by yourself Minor setbacks No danger and no harm Solutions are quick	Small Reactions Moaning Exhaling noisily Yearning Feeling let down Feeling discouraged	Examples Not doing your best on classwork Another day of indoor recess due to bad weather Your computer is "frozen" Your passed over for a lead role in a school-wide activity
Medium Actions (EFFECT 3-9 PEOPLE) May need to ask an adult for help No physical danger involved May take hours, days or weeks to resolve	**Medium Reactions** Feeling exasperated Feeling cross Feeling aggravated Feeling anxious Needing reassurance from others	**Examples** Unemployment of a family member Deployment or extended absence of a family member Power or water outage A relative moves in with your family
Large Actions (EFFECT 10+ PEOPLE) Resolved by many adults Involves danger and harm May take a long time to resolve	**Large Reactions** Feeling traumatized Feeling dazed Feeling stunned Feeling powerless Feeling helpless	**Examples** Natural disasters such as floods, tornadoes, hurricanes, earthquakes Civil unrest with physical altercations and destruction such as riots/protests War or terrorist attacks Plane, boat, train crashes

NAME ______________________________ DATE ________________

Thought Bubbles Worksheet

When ____
WRITE A BRIEF DESCRIPTION OF THE EVENT/SITUATION

____.

I thought …

The Girl with Negative Thoughts

Single-Minded Skunk

SEES THINGS IN
BLACK AND **WHITE** ...
GOOD OR BAD,
RIGHT OR WRONG

RIGID AND
INFLEXIBLE THINKER

General Ostrich

MAKES SWEEPING STATEMENTS

OVERSIMPLIFIES THINGS

USES WORDS LIKE
EVERYBODY, NOBODY,
ALWAYS, NEVER

STICKS HIS HEAD IN THE SAND
TO AVOID SEEING EXCEPTIONS

Filtering Flamingo

IGNORES SOME EVIDENCE
WHILE OVEREMPHASIZING
OTHER EVIDENCE

SIFTS, **SHADES** AND FILTERS
EVENTS TO ALTER REALITY

Count Batula

DISREGARDS THE POSITIVE

EXAGGERATES THE NEGATIVE

RIGHT OFF THE **BAT**, HE QUALIFIES ANY COMPLIMENTS HE RECEIVES

Leap Frog

JUMPS TO CONCLUSIONS

BELIEVES SHE KNOWS WHAT OTHER PEOPLE ARE THINKING

PREDICTS THE FUTURE

Labeling Leopard

THINKS EVERYTHING HAS A **SPOT** ...
SHE SORTS EVERYTHING AND EVERYONE INTO RIGID CATEGORIES

NEATLY LABELS EVERYONE AND EVERYTHING

Catastrophe Cat

THINKS OF THE WORST POSSIBLE SCENARIO

OVERREACTS AND BELIEVES PROBLEMS ARE INSURMOUNTABLE

ROUTINE SETBACKS BECOME **CAT**ASTROPHIC

Should Shark

BOLD AND INFLEXIBLE

USES WORDS LIKE
SHOULD AND **MUST**

MAKES OTHERS FEEL GUILTY,
FRUSTRATED, AND INADEQUATE

Badgering Badger

BADGERS AND NAGS CONSTANTLY

USES WORDS LIKE **SHOULD** AND **HAVE TO**

MAKE OTHERS FEEL GUILTY, FRUSTRATED, AND INADEQUATE

Fairness Falcon

OBSESSED WITH **FAIRNESS**

MAKES SURE THINGS ARE HANDLED IN A FAIR AND IMPARTIAL MANNER

BELIEVES HE ALONE IS THE TARGET OF INJUSTICE

HOLDS ONTO ANGER

Puffer Fish

SEES THINGS WAY
OUT OF PROPORTION

DOWNPLAYS OR
OVERPLAYS EVENTS

REALITY IS **PUFFED UP**
AND EXAGGERATED OR
UNDERESTIMATED

Dogmatic Dog

THE DOGMATIC DOG REPRESENTS
DOGAMATIC THOUGHTS

ALL 11 OF THE ANIMAL CHARACTERS HAVE DOGMATIC THOUGHTS THAT PLAY OVER AND OVER AGAIN IN THEIR MINDS

DOGMATIC THOUGHTS ARE INTRUSIVE AND DISRUPTIVE, LIKE A **BARKING DOG**

The Insidious Shadow

THE UNKNOWN AND AMBIGUOUS
"WHAT IFS" OF LIFE
PRODUCE **FEAR** ABOUT THE FUTURE

ANY ACTION
MIGHT MAKE THE
SITUATION WORSE

NAME ______________________ DATE ______________

Simple A.B.C. Worksheet

A **Actual Event:** What happened?

B **Belief or automatic thought:** What thoughts or images popped into your head?

C **Consequences:** How did you feel about what happened? How did you behave?

SCALING—RATE YOUR FEELINGS

MILD **1 . . . . . 2 . . . . . 3 . . . . . 4 . . . . . 5** STRONG

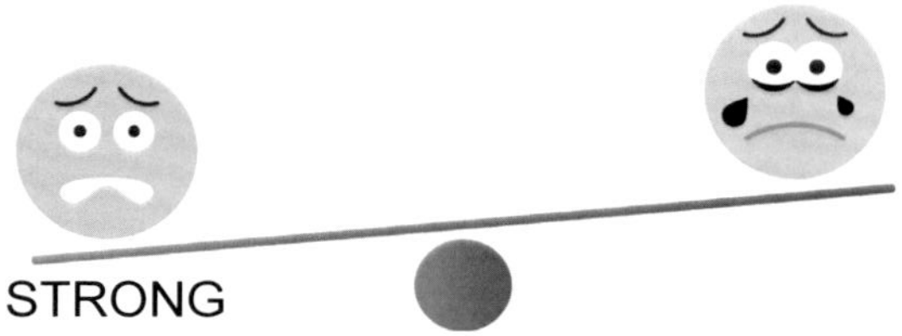

NAME ______________________ DATE ______________

A.B.C. Worksheet: Rethinking the Situation

A ACTUAL EVENT	B BELIEFS	C CONSEQUENCES		RETHINK THE SITUATION!
WHO? WHAT? WHEN? WHERE?	THOUGHTS	FEELINGS	PHYSICAL	ALTERNATIVE PERSPECTIVES
 What happened? Give details.	What thoughts or images popped into my head?  What meaning did I attach to my thoughts?	 What emotions did I experience? **SCALING** RATE YOUR FEELINGS 1.....2.....3.....4.....5 MILD STRONG	How did I behave?  What physical sensations did I experience?	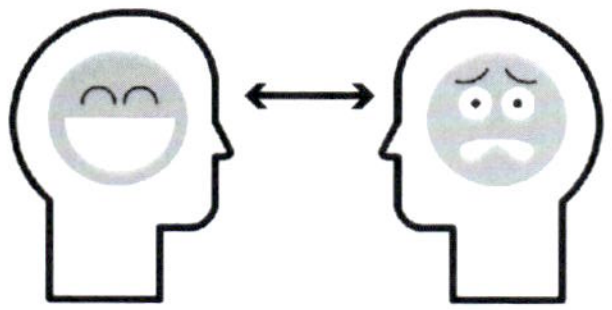 Is there another way of looking at the situation? Take a Google Earth view. What is the bigger picture? What advice would you give a friend if he or she was in a similar situation?

NAME ____________________ DATE ____________

A.B.C.D.E.F. Worksheet 1

A ACTUAL EVENT	B BELIEFS	C CONSEQUENCES		D DISPUTE	E EVALUATE	F FUTURE PLAN
WHO? WHAT? WHEN? WHERE?	WHAT WERE YOU THINKING?	HOW DID YOU FEEL?	HOW DID YOU REACT?	QUESTION YOUR THOUGHTS	SCRUTINIZE YOUR THOUGHTS	DO WHAT WORKS!
What happened? Give details.	What thoughts or images popped into my head? What meaning did I attach to my thoughts?	What emotions did I experience? **SCALING** Rate your feelings: 1…2…3…4…5 MILD STRONG	How did I behave? What physical sensations did I experience? Where did I feel those sensations in my body?	How important is this event? Is what I am thinking true? What else might be going on? How might this event be described in a different way? (GOOGLE EARTH VIEW) Is there something I should do less of or more of? What would others say about this situation?	What is causing me distress? Is my reaction in proportion to the event? Is what I am thinking a fact or my opinion? What is the best resolution for me? For others? For this situation? Are my ideas helpful? How does looking at this event from a different perspective make me feel?	What could I do differently? What strategies would be effective? What can I focus my time and attention on to help me feel better and gain balance? What things can I do that to help me cope more capably when faced with a distressing event? How could I respond to a similar situation in the future? **SCALING** Rate your feelings again: 1…2…3…4…5 MILD STRONG

NAME ______________________ DATE ______________________

A.B.C.D.E.F. Worksheet 2

A ACTUAL EVENT	B BELIEFS	C CONSEQUENCES		D DISPUTE	E EVALUATE	F FUTURE PLAN
WHO? WHAT? WHEN? WHERE?	WHAT WERE YOU THINKING?	HOW DID YOU FEEL?	HOW DID YOU REACT?	QUESTION YOUR THOUGHTS	SCRUTINIZE YOUR THOUGHTS	DO WHAT WORKS!
		SCALING Rate your feelings: 1…2…3…4…5 MILD STRONG				**SCALING** Rate your feelings: 1…2…3…4…5 MILD STRONG

STAND DOWN

What thoughts or images popped into my head?
↓
What am I feeling?
↓
What rating do I give the feeling?
↓
How am I behaving?
↓
What is happening inside my body?
↓
How important is this event/situation?
↓
Are my thoughts facts or just my opinion?
↓
Is there a different way of looking at this event/situation?
↓
What is the best resolution for this event/situation?

This is just a feeling … it will pass.
Take deep breaths. Count to 10.

DON'T BELIEVE *EVERYTHING* YOU THINK.

STAND DOWN

What thoughts or images popped into my head?
↓
What am I feeling?
↓
What rating do I give the feeling?
↓
How am I behaving?
↓
What is happening inside my body?
↓
How important is this event/situation?
↓
Are my thoughts facts or just my opinion?
↓
Is there a different way of looking at this event/situation?
↓
What is the best resolution for this event/situation?

This is just a feeling … it will pass.
Take deep breaths. Count to 10.

DON'T BELIEVE EVERYTHING YOU THINK.

NAME ____________________ DATE____________________

Pleasant ❤ Times

One good thing that happened is …	One thing I am looking forward to is …

CALM DOWN

STOP & STAND DOWN

Breathe
Count to 10 … *1 2 3 4 5 6 7 8 9 10!*
Go for a walk
Visualize or go to a quiet, calm place
Listen to music or read a book
Draw or paint
Write about your feelings
Exercise! Do yoga or jump rope
Talk it out

CALM DOWN

STOP & STAND DOWN

Breathe
Count to 10 … *1 2 3 4 5 6 7 8 9 10!*
Go for a walk
Visualize or go to a quiet, calm place
Listen to music or read a book
Draw or paint
Write about your feelings
Exercise! Do yoga or jump rope
Talk it out

Resources

Cognitive Behavior Therapy Resources

- Beck Institute for Cognitive Behavior Therapy – https://www.beckinstitute.org
- Get Self Help (free forms and worksheets) – https://www.get.gg/

Solution-Focused Brief Therapy Resources

- Solution-Focused Brief Therapy Association – http://www.sfbta.org/

Feeling Resources

Popular children's books that can be found in public and school library collections:

- *How Are You Peeling?* (Scholastic Book) by Saxton Freymann
- *The Feelings Book* by Todd Parr
- *The Way I Feel* by Janan Cain
- *The Feelings Book* (AmericanGirl™) by Dr. Lynda Madison

Workbooks/Lessons on feelings:

- *My Book Full of Feelings: How to Control and React to the Size of Your Emotions* by Amy Jaffe and Luci Gardner
- *Face Your Feelings* by Nicole Cleveland
- *Tough Enough to Cry* by Wanda S. Cook

YouTube™ has a wealth of free movies on the topic of feelings. Some of my favorites are:

- Inside Out Movie Clips – Get To Know Your Emotions by Disney Pixar Movie

Perspective Resources

Perspective and/or 3D optical illusion images can be found Online by searching for 3D optical images on perspective at Google Images™

Google Earth™ – free version